Second Journey

S.J. is the main character of this poetry book. Think of him as a compilation of Peter in "Peter Pan," who flies at will; Dorothy in "The Wizard of Oz," who walks the yellow brick road; or Temple Grandin, who knows how cows feel.

In this "Journey," S.J. can see, smell and hear what we can't. It's a fairy tale, a fantasy. Just indulge a little and give yourself a glimpse into this "Second Journey."

PREFACE

It was a seemingly endless dream. In his
nighttime fantasy, Second Journey (S.J.)
Cummings was born like a mainmast
topsail stretched in the gale with clear
senses: hearing, seeing, smelling; keener,
piercing, far reaching...

S. J. was never certain if he could trust
what W. B. Yeats said in his poem
"Second Coming": "Surely the Second
Coming is at hand." So, S. J. launched his
Second Journey.

It was exhausting as suddenly everything
everyone, every voice started to jam
his ears: small fish, enormous
elephants, flowers, birds, butterflies, dragonflies,
animals, leaves, trees, foliage, rain, sunshine,
paintings, mysterious souls, hidden
emotions, jealousy, vanity...

In addition, S.J. overheard love stories, rumors, gods' murmurings...; stumbled upon bragging, advice, lessons, warnings, preaching, enlightenment...

More than anything else, complaints, gripes and grievances...so tiresome. Therefore, S.J. fell deeply into so many dreams, reveries so often; in the trance, strange things transpired including the dialog with our Lord.

At the end, S.J. speaks out. In the spirit of "Every End Is My Beginning," S.J. plans to continue his journey, maybe someday he will meet "Ozymandias, King of Kings" or "a traveller from an antique land."

Poetry Books by Livingston Rossmoor*

A Stream Keeps Running (2013)

Do You Hear What I Sing (2014)

A Journey in the Animal Kingdom (2014)

A Never-Ending Battle (2015)

When Ruby Was Still in My Arms (2015)

I Hear the Ocean Landing (2016)

The Thunder Was So Mad (2017)

I Found Ruth Tonight (2017)

Collected Triplets (2018)

Selected Ballads, Villanelles, Couplets,
Tanka Sequences, Cinquains & Triplets (2018)

Selected Sonnets (2018)

Selected Poems 2002-2017 (2018)

Heart's Thread (2020)

Persephone's Spring (2020)

Rumi Inspiration (2021)

Odysseus's Odyssey (2021)

Selected Villanelles (2021)

A Man on the Tightrope (2022)

Second Journey (2022)

*For details, please visit www.livingstonrossmoor.com

Second Journey

Poems by Livingston Rossmoor

Published by
EGW Publishing
(Since 1979)

For my 3 children:
Emily, Gary and Wendy.

Thanks to Lisa Rigge, Charles Sandler,
Andy Shinkle and Chris Slaughter for
reviewing this compilation of poetry. I also wish
to thank Chris Slaughter for the organization
and production of this book.

EGW Publishing (since 1979)

ISBN: 978-0-916393-56-4

www.livingstonrossmoor.com

I am indebted to the editors who published my poems:

"Do chase the ebbing Neptune" received an Honorable Mention in the First Annual 2021 Nebraska Poetry Society Open Poetry Contest.

"Temptations" was previously published in "The Lyric" 2022.

Life is not measured by the number of breaths we take,
but by the moments that take our breath away.

Maya Angelou

TABLE OF CONTENTS

CHAPTER I
The Birth of S.J. Cummings

The Birth of S.J. Cummings
(Second Journey Cummings)

The circus left town, curtain falls, lights out.
No role to play, not even clowns, the show is over.
Everything dies down.

Sun seems too bright? Too dazzling?
Breeze too soft? Rains too little? Nights too dark?

Voice too faint?
Hearing, a guessing process,
fumbling through brain
spitting out words to make a sentence.

Ever had an ordeal
that guts out any motion and momentum?
Obliterates motivation, annihilates any hope?
Like a torpedo shattering the mettle,
unsettled the bearings,
sank the ship to the deepest ocean.

Ever witness a miracle?
The reconstruction of the wounded soul?
Through years and decades of dark period,
with a toolbox of unknown parts and pieces,
the ship is patched and amended, afloat again.

Determined to set sail
with a map of previous wreck, wrest and missteps,
back from the abyss, wind or no wind,
the second voyage stamped on the skin,
branded in the marrow.

S.J. Cummings was born like a mainmast topsail
stretched in the gale with clear senses:
hearing, seeing, smelling;
keener, piercing, far reaching.

For the Moment

S.J. watches the falling autumn leaves enjoying the moment.

Leaves falling in autumn,
tilted up by the wind pumping underneath,
swirling higher for an instant,
expectations running high,
every reason to begin appreciating
the beauty of the world:
bond, love, holding hands,
for the moment,
no doubt, the wind behind the sail,
tailwind forever,
for the moment an exultation
bursts in the singing,
rustles in the breeze,
counting the breaths and blessings,
uplifts the instant
for a modicum of
new height.

Impatiens

S.J. learns impatiens have something to say.

I never ask for much,
crumb, leftover will do.
Let them open their hearts
face to face,
talking to sun every day,
soaking, taking in all the glory.
I do not know if that pleases them,
I always suspect it won't,
if they realize they can't block and seize it all.

I do not know how
intermittent lights find their way
through layers of thick barriers to reach me.
Maybe they know,
I am forever waiting
under the branches and bough.

In the Garden

S.J. loitering in the garden.

In the garden you're allowed to cry a little,
touch where it hurts, see a light;
no wrinkles to smooth,
no stress to fret...

The end of the pier stretches into the ocean,
blanketed by white petals of clouds,
large lobs of dusky brume,
all swallowed into a chunky whiteness.
Meanwhile, camels plod through the desert,
curlews travel shore to shore to find home,
wild geese honk to remind the forthcoming of bitter winter.
The old groping for words to shake off the pang
of lingering weariness;
the young following Sisyphus,
pushing the boulder up the hill.

A Dream Named Longing

S. J. strolls to the pond in the fading sunset.

"Where are you?" some loons wail.
Silhouettes of trees, "I am here,"
bits of daylight left in the dale,
and the lake is so calm. "You'll hear,"
a distant voice: "and you will feel, loud and clear."

A song of untamed exploration,
so far away, so nearby,
a reminiscence of aspiration.
The haunting call, the perpetual cry,
exhaust every search, far and nigh.

It actualizes the soul's longing,
in touch with abandoned dream,
forsaken desire, a sense of belonging,
an echo of unyielding scream,
like loons' yodeling in the lingering gleam.

*Temptations**

S.J. meets one fisherman while he talks to the fish that is being set free.

The fat, round sunfish did not answer,
swam away when caught and released.
Baby bass opened his wide mouth,
hanging still while being unhooked,
I know he was listening.
The little one hiding in the seaweed,
twisted, jumped and
splashed into the shallow water,
he did not join the party.

Do not be fooled again by the moving worm!
Watch for that hiding hook!
This world is full of bait!
How many times before you learn!

*Previously published in "The Lyric" 2022.

Do I Know You?

In the woods near the pond, S.J. overhears someone's murmuring
with a stranger. At times, it sounds like a rather calm grumbling....

It seems you know me quite well,
like shadow following me.
Sometimes, I thought I heard a voice,
someone threw a pebble,
bounced couple times on the surface,
then sank soundlessly into the lake.

You never stop knocking,
like woodpecker, keeping at it,
always finding a way to din and sidle through.

Last night, you came after the second bounce.
I tried to catch you,
but you did not reach the shore.

I will be back,
with a net, a bucket, a fishing pole.

I know you always come.
I will wait.
This time,
I will wait.

CHAPTER II
Still You Dream

Going Home

Out of deep woods, in a trance, S.J. has a reverie on a sunny day.

Over the horizon, a shining ray of light
overwhelms my sight.
Behind the pinkish white, the yellow hue
hiding in the beige clouds,
a tiniest dot below,
a brown grayish island within the scope;
through the winding road,
circling down the mountain,
blue roof, green awning,
red umbrella table on the patio.
Fishing boats, sailing yachts,
pier, harbor,
sunny days,
a mother holding her boy's hand,
strolling in the sunset,
going home.

Voices

S.J. is still in a daydream; comes and goes, like the wind just passing through.

Out of total silence,
like the owl staring over your shoulder,
denying your existence,
like that trout just being set free,
whatever the claim,
goes back to where they came from;
like the deer looking at you,
when you start to pay attention,
she knows what is coming
and veers away;
like the wind,
just passing through.

44

Still You Dream

Dream after dream, S.J. was awakened by this dream.

Burn the box all the dirt.
Burn the box all the smears.
Burn the box all the tricks.
Burn the box all the traps.
Burn the box all the debts.
Burn the box all the lies.
Burn the box all the theories.
Burn the box all the beliefs.
Burn the box all the burdens.
Burn the box all the yokes.
Burn the box all the sweets.
Burn the box all the bitternesses.
Burn the box all the glories.
Burn the box all the wounds.
Burn the box all the regrets.
Burn the box all the sorrows.
Burn the box all the arguments.
Burn all the boxes,

just keep one;
keep the bird singing,
trust the dream,
envisage the finale,
await the melody.

I Do Not Blame You

In the fall, S.J. faces the roaring of the whole mountain at Franconia Notch.

No one cares if I'm a crabapple,
kousa dogwood, sassafras, spicebush,
or quaking aspen, black gum, shagbark hickory,
or river birch, sugar maple...

I do not blame you,
only one life,
you all come and go.

Through turmoil, all the chaos,
you come to see me.
You insist to capture the color
before it's all rotten in the soil,
blanched,
drifting in the wind.

For you, a chance to hear
the whole mountain
roaring at you.
For a moment,
wash away the dust you carry,
the yoke burdening your only life.
Such a short one.
I do not blame you.

Foliage

Around the pond, S.J. witnesses again the coming of fall foliage.

You are everywhere.
The hedges I can reach,
the sky covered by your branches.
I walk, I drive.
I want to catch first drop of dew.
I want to see more of you.

You love to surround the pond.
This morning,
you check, you look;
a little red here, purple there,
with the matching shirt,
and you never forget to don
your orange-yellow skirt.
Staring at the mirror of the tranquil water,
you sense the replica of your creation,
praying for Venus's help like Pygmalion,
or Narcissus, in love with your
own self-image.

I go to bed early.
Tomorrow,
I want to see,
how the first rays of dawn,
talk you into
putting on
daubs of golden honey,
and the dusky sunset convinces you
adding maroon and burgundy.

Elephant and Zookeeper

A good day at the zoo, S.J. listens to an elephant's lament.

My ancestors were everything but slaves;
they lifted heavy loads,
they moved logs from the woods to the river bank.
Under boiling sun, through rugged trails,
they battled in the war, their tusks against spears,
their noses ensnared, crushed all enemies.
Through muggy swamps,
my ancestors led the attack,
charged like tanks,
warriors bided behind their brawny legs,
my forefathers were the pillars of the village.

I followed their footsteps.
But now, my life is easy and lazy,
walking around inside the fence,
the keeper feeds me cabbage, lettuce, sugar cane,
apples, bananas...
No more work, just stare as onlookers gawk
while I crack peanuts without breaking the seeds.

51

Zookeeper's predecessor lived in Africa,
same as my ancestors.
She wore the same safari clothes every day.
She knows my glorious past,
toiled, trudged in the mud,
conquered the whole continent.
She should know I'll not break away,
no need to fence me,
no more territory for me to triumph over.

I do not complain; peanuts in my mouth,
chains clamped to my feet.
By now she knows I am not a slave, just retired.
In and out of cages, mine is the biggest one.

*She must have seen enough chains and cages,
since back in Africa, through "Middle Passage,"*
and now in the zoo, and go home to another cage.
In the meantime, sky hit the hay early
in the cold snowy day,
"Dark Symphony,"** marches on,
Satchmo's horn still setting soul on fire.*

*"Middle Passage" by Robert Hayden
**"Dark Symphony" by Melvin Tolson.

Cry Silences Cry

Out on the street, S.J. harkens to a cry at night.

Neon lit all night;
red, blue, stunning white,
pulses of the city,
dances of the street.
Wavering in their gazes,
harsh, dried-out shrill,
sobbing, withdrawn in the corner.
Reluctant to submit,
salvages the remaining insistence.
Door shuts,
knocking continues.
Pain numbs pain,
cry silences cry.

S.J. is bewildered in front of an unknown painting.

Every reference was linked to hit the heart,
the nucleus of the mystery,
epic center of the oscillation.
Broken dots, shaken twine;
zig, zag, up and down,
penetrating through the whole canvas,
punctuating the dots,
highlighting the lines,
invisible stripes,
in and out of memory,
flashing away, coming back,
multiple directions,
masks the trace, scratches the mark,
brushes every remote guidepost
towards the rim, in a circle,
regardless of colors,
round and round,
back to the center.

CHAPTER III
Every End Is My Beginning

Another Rose

S.J. sympathizes with rose's sour talk.

You always look at my thorns,
you have to touch them,
and feel you're still capable of
bringing back a load of grime,
coupled with those excruciating pairing lessons;
suffering, moaning...a complete cycle of preaching.
And then you withdraw your smile,
replace it with a refined leer and smirk,
pretend you are satisfied,
without even taking a look at me.

Scented Geraniums

Not only rose, some scented geraniums want their voices heard.
These fragrant plants offer an array of aromas: rose lemon, lime,
nutmeg, ginger, or chocolate scents.

I don't know why you care that much about the scent.
I don't know where it came from,
or why or when I own or lose it.
Your wine connoisseur bouquet-nose
picks me apart one scent at a time.
That seals your judgement,
without even looking at me.

Poinsettia

During the holidays, S.J. takes it to heart when poinsettia speaks out.

Centuries and centuries after,
it took a little girl, an ambassador, to spot
the stars on my petals.

This season, I am next to Him during Matins.
He saw me at Vespers.

Yesterday's dust on the leaves in the wild,
this morning's dew reflects the light.
Blake touched Him in "a Grain of Sand."*
Sexton felt "a great weight hung on a small wire."**

I heed enough prayers on the door step,
near the altar, under the trees.
It hasn't changed,
all of it matters to you;
how you find the Ariadne string,
escape the Labyrinth,
and discover your Golden Fleece.

*"Auguries of Innocence," poem by William Blake.
**"Small Wire," poem by Anne Sexton.

It Takes a Lot of Faith

When someone tells S.J. this story, he realizes this must be the first journey.

Who were you?
Distorted, squeezed my body and thorns into a circlet,
And who dared put me on the head of Jesus?
What was your intention?
Mocking authority, causing pain?
I was your symbol to cast more grief, derision
on every bloody, heavy-burdened, small step.

I carried your vile intent since then,
a long journey; Mount Zion, Jerusalem,
Constantinople, Byzantium, England, France...
I was preserved as a relic,
gilded with gold
to cover up the gory stain.

Your crime, forgiven; like countless others.
Just look at how peaceful I lived
in the Notre Dame Cathedral;
and how grateful I was,
when Father Fournier rescued me
from that blazing horrible fire.
(My new home is the Louvre museum.)
I am telling you all this,
still I do not know who you were?
Human is human.
Almost 2,000 years have passed,
evil becomes a footnote, a reminder, a reference;
pain, suffering, metamorphosized into honor, glory,
gratitude, joy and passion.

Enclosed, locked up,
confined into little circle
that I called home,
lived with every thorn of my own for 20 centuries,
it takes a lot of faith.

Every End Is My Beginning

S.J. thought first journey is some journey, but wow! This one is massive!

So much to tell you.
Where to begin?
Long, long time ago,
I came from a far, far away place,
sun rose from the East.
Helios drove his chariot from east to west.
East to West, I travel too.
Every step of the way;
burning moment, lame silence,
I wrote it on every seed inside my caves;
caves, yes it reminds me
once Persephone was kidnapped,
from sunshine world to the underworld.
Demeter must be very unhappy,
when she saw Hades holding me in his hand.
Proserpina regretted all her life eating my seeds.
It was all my fault, blood all over,
acrid, astringent, compromised sweetness at the end.

It is a long history,
someone counting my every seed,
Judaist insisted the total is 613,
a long list of Torah commandments to abide,
one seed at a time.
Pray, pray, pray,
one bead at a time.
King Solomon inscribed me
onto the columns of the holy temple he built.
Scouts brought me back to Moses,
confirmed the fecundity of the Promised Land.
More seeds, more offspring,
ingrained in my womb,
cushioned in my pulp,
comforted in my chambers.

Either my complexities captured your imagination,
or your imagination germinated my complexities;
symbols, meanings, implications
ascribed to every part of my body:
fertility, love, birth, rebirth, resurrection;
death, eternal life, marriage, abundance;
good, evil, bitter, desire, sin, suffering...
A full load of encumbrances,
the aspirations of human spirit,
unanswered questions,
from Judaism to Christianity, Buddhism,
Zoroastrianism, Islam and Hinduism;
embedded in the cultures of
Persians, Jews, Greeks, Indians, Chinese...

I carried for you all
throughout the millennia,
under the starlight,
blistering heat, freezing sleet,
from the dawn of human history,
until now.

So, slow down!
Before you crack me apart,
break my heart,
I want to tell you,
too old, maybe I am,
too tired, maybe I am,
still,
I am counting every mission
I carried out for you.

Beginning to the end.
Every end is my beginning.

CHAPTER IV
I Cry Often at Night

The Rain Came Late Last Night

S.J. is astonished every grievance strives for its own way to vent, eventually.

It is hard to please you.
You always think I am hiding somewhere,
picking my time to show up.

There are so many things I have to negotiate,
conflicts to settle.
You always think, just like in your office,
twist couple knobs, same temperature will be kept.

You always think I am just lucky;
share my sorrow, shed my tears;
street, alley, roof, basement, hill, beach.....
someone always listens to my muttering,
howling, outcrying at times,
outbursts at will;
and with such a blessing,
someone else always takes care of the debris
washed up by my down pouring.

73

Oftentimes, you needed my company,
and I was not there.
Or, I came
when you did not want to listen to my moaning.
And you continue to doubt if I have a heart.

The point is,
if you start to treat me like a human being,
maybe, maybe someday,
you will know the answer.

For You

S.J. knows that it is a foregone truth, there is no free lunch.
Everyone demands something in return.

For you
I sing songs arias
I play violin piano sonatas concertos
I read stories
I summarize
I analyze
I tell you my best assessment my honest opinion
I heighten your expectation
I give you advice
I calm your heartbeat
I soothe your blood flow
I am on call
I shut up at your command never complain

In the morning
Before bed
You listen
Keep on listening

You took it all in
Where did it all go
One of these days
Perhaps I will hear from you

Light

Finally, some bulbs over S.J.'s head shed some light.

Over your head,
I watch the pressure cooker,
beef stew....
spare rib curry....
carrots, potatoes, onions...
simmering, burbling in tiny bubbles,
learning to keep warm with their own tenderness,
speaking to each other,
spreading that affection with intimate conversations.

A rare agreement, right away,
you want to see what I see.
I think that was how
Hephaestus built the pot,
cooked up ambrosia
for the Olympians.

There Will Be Plenty of Silence

Strangely enough, S.J. encounters two flowers chatting with each other.

There is still time,
you try to tell me.
You were right when you told me,
on borrowed time we stay.

I used to hear birds singing,
winds blowing,
and narcissus flowering.

For you,
there was nothing but sandstorms,
searing sun,
oasis is a mirage.

Last night you flowered,
pinkish red budding in the dim light.
And I found my life in that new corner.
A long time to acquaint the darkness and faint light;
breathe, smell, recycle that dead air.
My tiny, yellowish, little bitty hearts cling together,
rowing, floating inside the white petals.
One heart scrounging from the other
and others,
stretching out the grief of soul;
deplore, despair cannot deprive the existence.

Or rather,
like the lonely you,
just a single bud.
Yet you said,
there will be plenty of silence
to find peace.

Wisteria

This is not just a gripe. S.J. is dumbfounded to realize wisteria is taking on the big media.

I remember you tried to tell me.
But I did not pay attention,
until I saw you everywhere;
in the air, on the printed pages,
on the video, TV,
your hands are everywhere.

Yet you report I am the one who steals the show,
if untrained, I could overwhelm the entire cosmos,
tangle up every human being.
And you claim at times I may be poisonous:
causing vomit, diarrhea, upset stomach,
while I barely climb over fences, gates,
hang around eaves.

I envy the skill you built up in every case,
without expressing an opinion,
you dissolve and deny
everyone's will to discover the truth.

80

While you know,
all I want is to have my own castle.
I love those walls, railings,
balustrades, awnings, canopies;
such a design for the roof,
chimney, window;
porch, balcony and gazebo.

You really do not need to target me.
I love such a variety of colors;
white, lilac, lavender, mauve,
purple, light blue, rich pink,
pale violet, deep violet...
even black, yellow, brown,
I love them all,
there is no one single true color.
You really do not need to be afraid,
do you?

I Cry Often at Night

What a lucky pattern, clear sunshine in the morning, all is beautiful;
after several nights, S. J. still hears a cry.

Boreas knows.
I cry often at night.
You never notice.
I may not come to your dream,
just let it drain and dry.
You always choose to wait it out
till sunrise.
You assume if you spend enough time
thinking it through,
the truth will surface under the sun.
Tears, confession mean nothing.
The light will ease the burden,
efface the unhappy past.

CHAPTER V
For There I Was

Augury

S.J. gets an earful of utterances.

You alone can block the sun.
No one holds you liable.
You always squeeze first,
then release.
You think constriction serves a meaning
to the impaired soul,
the release is a generosity
we all need to appreciate.

You do not understand the language:
oblivion, amnesia, abyss or Heaven.
Like Kronos kept trying back,
a complex issue,
he refused to be tightened,
in a pressing moment
death is accelerated,
acceptance is a mercy.

Again and again,
I call your attention to postpone the conclusion.

A Thread

S.J. takes a nap on the couch.

I know you come often,
same time every day.
You wish you were like me,
come and go,
missed by everyone
when I do not show up.

I am not a magician,
I climb to your window
brick by brick,
panel by panel, inch by inch...
then I retreat to my darkness.
But never Dark Triad again.
We need to hold on to some light;
some magical spell;
some name their babies
Adonis, Artemis, Persephone, Lucifer, Titan...

Invent a name, a wonder,
create a space, a thread.

Rumors

In broad daylight, S.J. pays attention to a series of rumors from a
whistleblower.

I
Do not cry for Eurydice. Hey, Orpheus,
maybe she'd rather live in the underworld.
Persephone too,
she picks the flowers she likes,
Hades built her a garden,
loves her faithfully,
and they lived happily thereafter.

II
Not like his brother Zeus,
ruler of sunny days, twinkling nights.
Hera going after Zeus' lovers,
day and night.

III
And you,
you are targeted.
Not just you.
All in the file.
There is no escape from prophecy.
The writing's on the wall,
in the book;
every trace,
every movement,
every route, pattern,
every vision, inspiration, aspiration,
every thought,
every thirst,
every need,
every want,
every smile,
every frown.

IV
Trees, unfettered to grow,
pine, oak, blade of grass,
shrubs, sedges, flowers...
birds, free to fly,
they choose their own routes;
woodpeckers din as they wish,
osprey swoops down to catch fish.
Circling hawk seeks his moment,
zooms in to snap the fleeing mouse.
Butterflies, bees, hummingbirds
rule their own lives;
live and die,
die and live
at will.
The envy of everyone,
not just Tithonus.

Color

This is not the first nor the last time S.J. hears someone's boasting.

You never stop bragging how unique,
how beautiful you are.

But at the end,
your life **summed** up in my color.
No difference than the one next to you.

All the rasp against the panoply of truth;
a foil to uncover the fact;
the sane and insane verity.

Through all their trepidation,
blind opulence and gluttony
still dominate.
All the vagrants rebel against pompousness,
in vain.

There was time I held my head up,
dressed in something deep.
But not now,
return to chastity;
pure and simple.

At the end,
we all go back to the beginning,
with the same color.

I Survive

S.J. confronts Ms. J., but she insists "I Survive."

Young, old, very old,
throughout generations,
past, present, future;
the world is my playground.
Where are you from?
Oftentimes you ask me.

Once I thought I lived in the sky,
so lofty, any form I like:
angular, square, cube, spiky,
cylinder, triangle, crown-shape, bubble-like...
anytime,
I can dissolve into thin air,
into every breath,
buffet any cheeks.

Once you thought,
only in that moment, intoxicated,
but I prevailed in perpetuity.
You think you are free of me;
yet you embrace and smile,
pretend no bitterness,
no whimper, bile nor snivel;
you think,
once you succeed with semblance of triumph,
glory sinks into the marrow of your bones;
dancing, beaming,
surrounded by flashy butterflies,
iridescent wings,
no more buzzing, tingling, stinging bees.
You think you got rid of me,
until you sense I am still here.

I survive every feeling:
cry, laughter, sorrow,
joy, jubilance;
heart-broken tragedy,
anger, despair;
ardor, envy, enthusiasm,
tranquility;
prayer, enlightenment...
I survive every emotion of mankind.

For There I Was

S.J. meets up with Mr. Hevel, and finds out he lives closer than next-door neighbor.

Not long ago, I lived in the deep sea;
mysterious creatures,
terrifying faces:
fang tooth, blobfish, stargazer,
goblin shark, black swallower.....

I hid my breath,
in the dead quiet,
I could hear Hades' pulse,
another entrance?
Not Attika Parnes Mountains,
nor Lake Avernus.
Where was I?
Near Lethe or Styx?

Throughout the day,
I groped through obscurity,
grappled to grab, grasp and grip;
piles and piles of weed, algae,
I dug deeper into the gloomy space,
sank to the bottom.
A constant challenge to stay dormant.

In a heartbeat, more often than not,
I heard the call,
I popped, propelled all the way to the surface,
stirred up the waves,
raising the fight against the seemingly calming winds.

I found myself again,
my home under a tissue.

Once I wondered;
where is my home?

For there I was.

CHAPTER VI
I Carry the Monarch on My Wings

I Carry the Monarch on My Wings

Once upon a time, S.J. unearthed a love story.

I know where you are.
From the day I was born I looked for you.
You told me you'll always wait for me.

Bulldozer engulfed your village,
your home became a victim.
I kept looking.

You may think I gave up, vanished.
Even I am chosen, in Elysian Fields,
My son, son's son; daughter, daughter's daughter
will continue looking for you.

I told them how beautiful you are,
your welcome bouquet comes in many colors:
rose-purple, white with purplish centers,
magenta red, pink, bright orange, yellow-orange,
pale-greenish, tinged maroon...
you are humorous with funny faces,
whorled, antelope-horns;
subdued like common folk,
showy like a star...
and you live humbly,
in the shade, near swamp, prairie
and desert too.

Not like Circe's potion,
they can drink your nectar,
stay for a couple days or weeks.
Not like Calypso,
you would never hold them hostage
for months, years.

Decades, centuries gone by,
now sun is testing our limits,
so is cold air, drought and fierce wildfire.
It takes four, five generations to
cross the borders.
I carry the monarch on my wings.

"Do chase the ebbing Neptune"*
S.J. meets a person who is still chasing the ebbing Neptune

It must be a mistake.
I thought it was a promise,
you would be the last one
left without saying goodbye.
You said it all comes and goes.
When all are gone,
I can dig and dig
like the sandpipers chasing the beach crabs.

It was a turbulent storm,
the night you arrived,
you drew a line in the sand
and swore you would come again.

This morning, I hurried back,
the line disappeared,
I dug and dug, not there.
At night,
when the moon was half bright;
in the dark, no trace, no sign.

106

Day, night, I went back;
new lines, old lines,
crossed my heart,
smudged, blurred my eyes,
storms, waves, ripples...
pounding, slapping, murmuring.

You were not the only one
drew a line through my name.

O God, everything is just water,
swallow, spit it out, let it go,
cry out loud,
I heard it again and again.

Still, I keep going back when
sun rises or
moon's behind the moonlight.

*Received an Honorable Mention in the First Annual
2021 Nebraska Poetry Society Open Poetry Contest.

Don't Break the Staff

S.J. hears the tree talking to someone. But S.J. cannot find anyone around.

You walk by me every day.
No hello, no greeting,
you know I know you well.

A struggle to keep your back straight,
not this morning,
head down into chest,
eyes losing focus,
and you stop beside me,
trying to recall something.

I remember those days,
you walked and talked to yourself,
hands, arms motioned with gestures,
pointing, launching into a soliloquy,
I can hear the voices too.
Not today.
You are tired and it is only morning.

All you were thinking was how to say good-bye.
A long list to tighten, justify;
issues yet to uncover.
How did you get here? Where to go?

Do you really want to know?

I am not on your list,
because I am always here.

And I know what tired you the most.
Like Pericles, who once thought
he lost his beloved daughter and wife.
"A man who for this three month hath not
spoken to anyone, nor taken sustenance."

Questions, answers,
It used to be so simple.

Dead tree trunks stuffed with acorns.
Raindrop-laden daffodils take a bow.
Bluebirds drink rain water,
jump around the old oak tree.

Hopping, dancing, along with the miracle:
Pericles reunited with Marina and Thaisa.

We "were all spirits and
Are melted into air, into thin air;"

"Let your indulgence set me free."
Prospero ended his epilogue.

Break, break,
don't break the staff.

Helios at High Noon

S.J. does not plan to eavesdrop, but somehow he intercepts Helios'
self-talk.

I had to rub my eyes to make sure
it was you, I saw.
In the middle of the day,
sitting on the doorstep.

Busy was I, still I noticed,
you had remained there for half a day.
Looking at me?

I knew it was not me.
Farther, higher beyond me
you stared.

Why still remember I?
If you check my calendar,
I am occupied every minute, every hour.
I know you work the same way.
You were so focused, executed by the book,
wasted not a minute,
and there you sat for hours
and hours.

111

Something happened?
Broken? Lost completely? Everything gone?
No place to turn to?
What to do next?

If I cannot keep up,
I'll call Apollo to take over.

Maybe that is why I still remember you.

CHAPTER VII
Another Prophet's Advice

Come, Come, Before They Come

S.J. knows this is coming, not a surprise. California poppies are everywhere. S.J. is bound to hear from poppies more than once. What is unexpected this time is that the California poppies are not just swaggering, but also lecturing.

You think you know what I know
Still you see
Monarch butterflies in Carmel
Half-naked bodies on sunny beach
California poppy in Antelope valley

I am coming
Flowers flowers
Mountain Valley Ranch
Poppy poppy
State Park National Park
Desert beach
Wild wild
Camera clicking
Go go
Before caterpillars eat them all
I keep coming
You think you know what I don't

Mojave poppy
Canterbury bells
Desert dandelion
Know what you don't
Near beach
Hyacinth
Morning glories
Baby blue eyes
Know much more

Popcorn flowers
Tidy tip
Sunups
Know even more
Sky lupine
Up the hill
All the way
To the sky

Fire will come wind will gust
Sky will turn orange air will smell
Run run you will be on the run

You think I am just lucky
Show up at the right time
Disappear when you suffer

You forget I was eaten
Trashed
Burnt to death
You shall know by now
I will come again
In the meanwhile
Come come
Before they come
"also rejoice in our sufferings,"

When time begins
"suffering produces perseverance;"

When time ends
"perserverance, character;
character, hope."

Dragonfly

Now, once it started, haranguing never ends. This time, it comes
from a tiny dragonfly.

Don't ask me about my history.
I do not have a shining past.
There is nothing much I can tell you, except
for four years I lived as a wingless nymph,
shedding skin, changing look, fifteen times.

You may say I learned to sacrifice,
survive; enshrouded, biding my time.
Or yes, everyone lives through grime and slime.

Yet everyone is blessed with just one single stage,
I prepared four years for this only moment.
Yours could take 40 years or more to build up.
I do not know about you; for me,
I don't like to talk about the past,
a drawn-out colloquy would suck all my energy.
But now, more than anything else,
I am so glad, I can show you my best.
Finally, I can fly with my ultimate make up;

dress like a princess,
brilliantly iridescent in the sunlight,
dance with pursuing princes.
Everyone can see me,
conspicuous with metallic colors.
It lasts for a few days; or a couple weeks,
maybe months, at the most.
I fly from meadow to meadow, pond to pond.
I rest from stalk to stalk, rock to rock.

"Then what?" You ask.

I enjoy every minute,
from moment to moment,
then die, a crystal clear ending,
not a dragging process.
I save the best for the end.
How about you?
Have you prepared for the moment?
Do you know what I mean, moment to moment?
Not a protracted mechanism,
not just the ongoing sunrise, sunset,
but the best for the moment, now.

Beyond Nazareth

Lesson, lesson, lesson; S.J. has never been in Jerusalem, let alone Nazareth. But, somehow, he insisted someone from Nazareth gave him a tongue-lashing.

The arrow tries to be more than itself,
resists pressure, endures strain,
looking for the instant to be snapped,
released by the tension of bowstring.

More than self, is that a calling?
Exposes to the world, reveals all.
What comes next?
A wall, yes, a wall.

Hardly any believers in Nazareth.
A carpenter's son,
nothing beyond that.
Same quarters, same lot.

It's much, much more.
Three days changed the world order.
Go, go, beyond Nazareth,
where there's no border.

Until I Found You

This is not a lesson, more like an enlightenment. S.J. comes across a poet who apparently is in love with something.

So many things lost under my watch.
Like birds woke up and flew away.
Never know where they go,
except return no more.

As though some shadow behind me,
they hid and picked what they wanted,
what hurt me the most.

Like a sandcastle pilfered by incoming tides,
eroded, collapsed, all I could do was watch
as it was dismantled, dissipated, grain by grain.

I did not know how desperately
I was looking for something that
no one could take away,
until I found you.

123

Yes, life on Mars,
and of course the moon is just a colony,
the hidden secret in between,
interspersed by strata of the darkest universe,
that is where I found you.

Yes, morning dews evaporate,
but Eos always sends them back to sparkle.
In the gap,
Helios bounces sunshine in bright daylight,
brushes a lambent carmine in the dusky sky,
and in the vanishing sunset,
Selene urges the moon to part the hill,
that is where I found you.

And no one can ever take it away,
from me.

Another Prophet's Advice

All along, S.J. was hoping to meet a prophet. Finally, he receives
advice from one.

It is intimidating,
how many years more are needed.
Read, read, unlimited,
while forgetting everything you've read.
Odysseus never read,
all those years,
all those islands,
all those young goddesses,
all those stories he recited.
A decade of wars,
a decade of being lost;
failed, defeated, escaped,
unquestioned, unsuspected, unthwarted,
that is all he needed.
Beyond that,
forget not to come home.
Now, go back to scratch not just the surface,
dig a little deeper,
turn the stone,
unearth the worms...

Gone, Gone, Gone

*Boy, this is a serious matter, more than a lecture, preaching, advice,
enlightenment; someone sternly blasting out like Robinson Jeffers.*

We would surely live to the end of our lives. Our children will
feel the heat, still be able to do the same. Their children will
need the cover-up to block the higher heat. Their children's
children will need goggles and masks all day long like aliens
from Mars.

It would not take long to melt all the remaining icecaps and
glaciers in the Arctic. Polar bears are good swimmers,
penguins have no ice, no snow to waddle, no place to dig the
burrows for their babies. Ocean rises to flood Miami,
Manhattan, Shanghai, New Orleans...Nebraska becomes a
desert. Sandstorms, a daily battle.

We are approaching the tipping point; over this point, there
will be no return. We must wake up to the scientific evidence.
We must take action. Climate is not the enemy. Science is not
the enemy, we are our own enemy. The denial is the most
outlandish display of human stupidity. "There is not one
memorable person." As Jeffers said. The rising heat and
oceans will prove not just "no one is memorable," but also, at

the end, no one survives, let alone is memorable. Humans are all spoilers. Jeffers also said, "There is not one mind to stand with the trees, one life with the mountains." And from his poetry, we can add, there is not one courage with hawk, one nobility with lovely rock, one thought with water, one soul with air...

"Humans are too egocentric, detached from the beauty of nature, they are so unmoved by the 'astonishing beauty of things,'" these were words of Jeffers. Build, build, build; progress, progress, progress. Giant Ibis will bid goodbye soon, followed by California Condor, Philippine Eagle, Christmas Island Frigate...no hawk in sight at Hawk Tower. No one cares, silent spring is coming; no one cares; then fish, animals...; silence, silence, silence; only human noises, dried out rivers; desert, storm, flocks of human migrants.

Ignoring "astonishing beauty of things" is not a crime, invading the beauty of things is a sin. Water, air polluted in the name of progress. Bird, fish, animal, rock, tree, icecap, ice sheet, glacier, river...crime or no crime, no one cares. Progress, progress, progress; invasion, destruction, nuclear radiation, no one cares. Progress, progress, progress; atmosphere, earth, climate change, temperature blazing...no one cares.

127

Endangered species list is getting longer. They will soon all be
gone. Endangered plants, flowers, grasses...;
endangered rivers, seashore, beaches, water, air...;
gone, gone, gone. Now, endangered earth;
endangered human beings.

There should be no astonishment, no amazement, no
metaphor and no image. This is not just a poem, or an
emotional outburst.

Progress, progress, progress; no one cares, no one cares,
no one cares; gone, gone, gone.

CHAPTER VIII
Lord, My Lord

A Lone Wolf Howling at the Moon

S.J. has to admit, it is astounding to witness a lone wolf gazing and howling at the moon.

It lasts a long while, it lasts...
lingers in the mid-air,
perishes in silence...
Trying to find a friend to talk to?
Someone you can see every night?
Someone will not betray you?
A good listener, will not forsake?
Not like your buddy just got killed by a hunter,
or lover found her new love?
Nor like your enemy, hiding,
stalking to snap you,
to haunt you,
never let go of you.

You must be tired?
Trailing every track to the end of woods,
retreating to the rim of ridge, edge of cliff,
run, keep running, running away
from friends, enemies, lovers;
some loved you, some feared you,
some turned their backs against you.
Run, run,
evading the trap,
time and time again.

Watching every step,
eyes open, ears listening,
at night, the familiar light from
a true friend, the moonlight
caresses your face,
cuddles your shoulders,
cold and chill, covers you whole:
legs, tail, head and shadow.
Throughout the night,

she is patient, standing still, moves little,
just enough to let you know she is heeding,
never shouting back;
when she hides in the clouds,
you know she is there,
talking to you in the silence,
always there,
like your loneliest howl,
yearning,
longing,
halts,
pauses,
still there.

Lord, My Lord

S.J. thinks, it has been a long journey, maybe it is time to go to
church. So he does. He is so tired, he dozes off, dreams a longest
dream. When he wakes up, no one is there.

In my dream, I remember,
face to face with my Lord at the stern,
the sailing trail agitates the surface,
ruffles the ripples,
disappears into water
like fleeting bubbles in the froth.

He grins and asks me **"How have you been?"**
"I wish I can swim like a fish."
He says **"I can throw you back to the ocean**
and make you a fish."
"O Lord, but do not make me a shark,
with jagged teeth in my jaws,
do not make me a whale,
hunter's harpoons never fail,
do not make me a bluefin tuna,
for sale at Tsukiji auction to fetch the highest dollar,
do not make me a sardine,
millions squeezing into the tiny space,
breathing to death in each other's face."

136

"Instead I can throw you into the sky and make you fly."
"O Lord, but do not make me a hummingbird,
heeds gossip, dashes on every fickle mind,
hungry, thirsty, always in a bind,
do not make me a woodpecker,
pokes, knocks, warns and alarms, all in vain,
do not make me a vulture,
strips carcasses, stems bugs and disease,
a sanitary vigilante to no one's please,
do not make me a locust,
swarms, aggregates, drear in fear."

The veils in the air holding its breath, still and quiet,
as though we are the first to discover this strait.

"I can throw you back into the clouds."
"O Lord, but do not make me a drop of rain,
bringing dirt and dust back to the Earth,
do not make me a rainbow,
appearing only after the rain,
do not make me a morning dew,
perishing when the sky turns blue,
do not make me a dusky sunset,
rosy for a second, then comes darkness's threat."

Reefs, caves, berths and docks, along the inlet,
sand dunes on the shore, a bluff of woodland behind.

"I can throw you into the wild, back to the forest."
"O Lord, but do not make me a wolf,
running with the loneliest howling,
do not make me a sloth,
hugging the branch to death,
never lets go of the pining,
do not make me a dragon,
swims, flies, mighty miracle only in dreaming,
do not make me a thoroughbred,
trophies, records, un-ended yearning."

My Lord is a patient God.
**"There are no other choices then,
I'll just throw you back to the world."**
"O Lord, but do not make me a driver,
stuck in traffic, I'd rather be fishing in the river,
do not make me a messenger,
confounded in the muddy barrier,
do not make me a follower,
groping around the ivory tower,
do not make me a ruler,
I'd rather be a scholar."

All silence, the ship reaches the shore.

In my dream, I heard my own voice:
"O my Lord, one more, one last request, then
I'll ask not what God can do for me."

"What is that, my boy?"

"Lord, my Lord, descend from the blue,
but throw me back to your Heaven."

The Interlude

It was like a seemingly endless dream, when S.J. woke up, no one was there. So, he thought it would be a good time for a confession:

S.J. was never certain if he could trust what W.B. Yeats said in his poem "The Second Coming": "Surely the Second Coming is at hand." So Second Journey (S.J.) was launched, as this is a sure thing and definitely it is coming and taking place right now; he could singlehandedly make it happen. The journey is exhausting, the dream of "Lord, My Lord" might have dreamt too far and too far-flung. Fortunately, he was in the church, anytime is a good time to wake up.

In the spirit of "Every End is My Beginning," S.J. plans to continue his journey. Maybe someday he will meet "Ozymandias, King of Kings" or "a traveller from an antique land."

About the Author

This is Livingston Rossmoor's 22nd book. As of this writing, he has written and published 19 poetry books. Livingston has also written 2 books of prose and poetry, 1 book of 13 short stories and composed 21 lyrics and melodies collected in 2 DVDs and 1 CD. His poems have appeared in numerous publications: local newspapers, magazines, newsletters and overseas publications. In addition, Livingston's poems were published in *The Lyric, Poetry Quarterly, Ibbetson Street, California Quarterly* (California State Poetry Society), *Wisconsin Review, Loch Raven Review, Time of Singing* poetry journal and *Chronogram* magazine. Many of his poems were selected as honorable mentions in the following contests: *Writer's Digest Annual Writing Competition, California State Poetry Society Annual Contest* and *Nebraska State Poetry Society Open Poetry Contest*. One poem was awarded 3rd place in the *Annual Poetry Contest for the Dancing Poetry Festival*.

Livingston received his MS degree from UC Riverside and MA degree at UC Berkeley. Among his 40-plus year entrepreneur career,* he devoted many decades to publishing. Livingston oversaw the production of 12 printed consumer magazines and formerly served as the editorial director of the journal *Nourish-Poetry*. He is currently an associate member of the Academy of American Poets and a member of the California State Poetry Society.

Livingston resides in California with his dear wife. He has 3 children and 8 grandchildren.

*Livingston worked two jobs for 15 years to launch and build his various ventures; he was the founder, Chairman and CEO of four corporations at different stages of his business career in four fields: Radiopharmaceutical manufacture, real estate, software (SaaS) and publishing.

EGW Publishing
(Since 1979)

www.livingstonrossmoor.com

Made in the USA
Columbia, SC
07 December 2022

72357082R00088